D1174769

LANGSTON HUGHES

LET AMERICA BE AMERICA AGAIN

WOODCUTS BY ANTONIO FRASCONI

Published by
George Braziller, Inc.
171 Madison Ave.
New York, NY 10016
www.georgebraziller.com

LIBRARY OF CONGRESS CATALOGING IN PUBLICATION DATA

Hughes, Langston, 1902-1967.
  Let America be America again / Langston Hughes ; woodcuts by Antonio
Frasconi.
    p. cm.
  ISBN 0-8076-1550-1 (hardcover)
  1. America--Poetry. 2. Social problems--Poetry. I. Frasconi, Antonio.
II. Title.
  PS3515.U274 L8 2004
  811'.52--dc22

                    2004018497

DESIGN ASSISTANCE BY JERRY KELLY

PRINTED AND BOUND IN SPAIN

FOREWORD BY HENRY LOUIS GATES, Jr.

LANGSTON HUGHES, KNOWN THROUGHOUT HIS CAREER AS "SHAKESPEARE IN HARLEM," WAS THE MOST IMPORTANT AFRICAN-AMERICAN POET IN THE FIRST THREE QUARTERS OF THE TWENTIETH CENTURY. HUGHES WAS AS PROLIFIC AS HE WAS VERSATILE, WRITING 50 BOOKS BETWEEN 1925, AT THE HEIGHT OF THE LITERARY MOVEMENT KNOWN AS THE HARLEM RENAISSANCE, AND HIS DEATH IN 1967. HUGHES WAS A MASTER OF SEVERAL LITERARY GENRES, INCLUDING POETRY, THE NOVEL, ESSAYS, PLAYS, LITERARY AND MUSICAL CRITICISM, AUTOBIOGRAPHY, CHILDREN'S FICTION AND JOURNALISM. HE PUBLISHED 16 VOLUMES OF POETRY, TEN BOOKS OF SHORT STORIES, TWO NOVELS, TWO AUTOBIOGRAPHIES, NINE CHILDREN'S BOOKS AND MANY OTHERS. HE ALSO EDITED SEVERAL IMPORTANT ANTHOLOGIES AND PLAYED A PIVOTAL ROLE IN INTRODUCING THE WORK OF BLACK AFRICAN, CARIBBEAN AND LATIN AMERICAN AUTHORS TO AMERICAN READERS THROUGH HIS TRANSLATIONS FROM THE FRENCH AND SPANISH ORIGINAL OF THEIR WORK. THE QUALITY OF HIS WORK, ITS SHEER VOLUME AND HUGHES'S LONGEVITY, ALL HAVE CONTRIBUTED TO HIS STATUS AS ONE OF THE TRULY SEMINAL WRITERS THAT THE AFRICAN-AMERICAN LITERARY TRADITION HAS PRODUCED

JAMES MERCER LANGSTON HUGHES WAS BORN ON FEBRUARY 1, 1902 IN JOPLIN, MISSOURI, AND WAS RAISED PRIMARILY IN LAWRENCE, KANSAS. HUGHES'S FAMILY WAS EXTRAORDINARILY LITERATE; BOOKS AND THE DISCUSSION OF IDEAS PLAYED A FUNDAMENTAL ROLE IN HIS LIFE FROM CHILDHOOD. HIS MATERNAL GREAT-UNCLE, JOHN MERCER LANGSTON, ONE OF THE MOST PROMINENT AFRICAN-AMERICANS OF HIS TIME, PUBLISHED HIS AUTOBIOGRAPHY "FROM THE VIRGINIA PLANTATION TO THE NATION'S CAPITOL," IN 1894. HIS MOTHER, CARRIE LANGSTON, ATTENDED COLLEGE, WROTE POETRY AND PERFORMED DRAMATIC READINGS. HUGHES'S FATHER, JAMES NATHANIEL HUGHES, COMPLETED A CORRESPONDENCE COURSE IN LAW, ONLY TO BE DENIED THE RIGHT TO SIT THE BAR EXAMINATION IN THE OKLAHOMA TERRITORY BECAUSE HE WAS BLACK, LEADING HIM TO MOVE TO JOPLIN IN 1899. JAMES HUGHES WOULD MOVE TO MEXICO IN 1903, ABANDONING CARRIE AND 18-MONTH-OLD LANGSTON.

DESPITE THE FACT THAT PART OF HIS MOTHER'S FAMILY ENJOYED ECONOMIC SECURITY, CARRIE HUGHES DID NOT. SHE SOUGHT MENIAL JOBS IN A VARIETY OF CITIES OVER THE NEXT NINE YEARS, BOARDING LANGSTON IN LAWRENCE WITH HER MOTHER, MARY LEARY LANGSTON, WHO

SUPPORTED LANGSTON AND HERSELF BY RENTING ROOM TO STUDENTS AT
THE UNIVERSITY OF KANSAS. MARY LANGSTON WAS ONCE HONORED BY
PRESIDENT THEODORE ROOSEVELT AS THE ONLY SURVIVING WIDOW OF
JOHN BROWN'S RAID ON HARPERS FERRY. STILL, HUGHES'S EARLY YEARS WERE
ECONOMICALLY IMPOVERISHED, IF NOT IMPOVERISHED IN IMAGINATION.
"BOOKS," HE ONCE WROTE, "BEGAN TO HAPPEN TO ME." EVEN BEFORE
THE AGE OF SIX. HUGHES READ VORACIOUSLY AND AVIDLY, COUNTERING
THE POVERTY AROUND HIM WITH THE RICHNESS AND SPLENDOR OF
POETRY AND FICTION – "BOOKS," HE WOULD WRITE, " THE WONDERFUL
WORLD IN BOOKS."
        HUGHES'S MOTHER EVENTUALLY REMARRIED, AND HUGHES JOINED HIS
MOTHER AND STEPFATHER IN LINCOLN, ILLINOIS, BEFORE MOVING TO CLEVELAND,
OHIO, WHERE HE SPENT FOUR GLORIOUS YEARS AT CENTRAL HIGH SCHOOL.
HUGHES WAS A VARSITY TRACK ATHLETE, HE WAS AN HONOR STUDENT,
HE PUBLISHED POETRY IN THE SCHOOL'S LITERARY MAGAZINE AND HE
SERVED AS EDITOR OF HIS CLASS'S YEARBOOK. IT WAS IN HIGH SCHOOL
THAT HUGHES BECAME ENAMORED OF THE POETRY OF WALT WHITMAN,
CARL SANDBURG AND PAUL LAURENCE DUNBAR, WHO WOULD REMAIN

HIS PRINCIPAL INFLUENCES, ESPECIALLY SANDBURG'S USE OF FREE VERSE
AND WHAT HUGHES'S BIOGRAPHER, ARNOLD RAMPERSAD, HAS CALLED
"A RADICALLY DEMOCRATIC MODERNIST AESTHETIC."
        HUGHES'S CAREER AS A WRITER WAS LAUNCHED IN THE SUMMER
OF 1920, WHILE CROSSING THE MISSISSIPI RIVER BY TRAIN ON HIS WAY
TO VISIT HIS FATHER IN MEXICO. WRITING ON THE BACK OF AN ENVELOPE,
HUGHES COMPLETED A POEM THAT HE WOULD CALL "THE NEGRO SPEAKS
OF RIVERS." IT BECAME THE MOST VIVIDLY ANTHOLOGIZED POEM IN
AFRICAN-AMERICAN LITERATURE. HUGHES WAS 18 YEARS OLD; HE HAD
WRITTEN THE POEM IN 15 MINUTES. ITS FINAL STANZA READS:
        I'VE KNOWN RIVERS
        ANCIENT, DUSKY RIVERS

        MY SOUL HAS GROWN DEEP LIKE THE RIVERS.
THE RISE OF LANGSTON HUGHES'S LITERARY CAREER WAS METEORIC;
W. E. B. DU BOIS, THE FIRST AFRICAN-AMERICAN TO EARN A PH.D. FROM
HARVARD AND A FOUNDER OF THE N.A.A.C.P., PUBLISHED TWO OF HIS
POEMS IN HIS PERIODICAL, "THE BROWNIES' BOOK," IN JANUARY 1921 AND

A CHILDREN'S PLAY IN JULY. AN ESSAY AS WELL AS "THE NEGRO SPEAKS OF RIVERS" APPEARED IN THE JUNE ISSUE OF "THE CRISIS" MAGAZINE. ANOTHER DU BOIS PUBLICATION, THE OFFICIAL JOURNAL OF THE N.A.A.C.P. AND THE MOST WIDELY READ BLACK MAGAZINE IN THE WORLD. HUGHES, IT IS FAIR TO SAY, WAS A FAMOUS WRITER EVEN BEFORE HE ENROLLED AT COLUMBIA UNIVERSITY IN THE FALL OF 1921.

HUGHES HATED COLUMBIA, WITHDRAWING AT THE END OF HIS FIRST YEAR. IN THE SPRING OF 1923, HE SET SAIL BY FREIGHTER FOR AFRICA, WORKING AS A CABIN BOY. FAMOUSLY TOSSING HIS COLUMBIA ENGINEERING TEXT-BOOKS INTO THE ATLANTIC, SEEKING TO SHED AN IDENTITY THAT, HE FELT, HAD BEEN UNDULY ENFORCED BY HIS FATHER, HOPING THROUGH THIS ACT OF MOLTING TO CREATE FOR HIMSELF "A TABULA RASA" ON WHICH A NEW, SELF-DEFINED AND SELF-DIRECTED HUGHES-THE-WRITER COULD INSCRIBE THIS NEW SELF.

HUGHES TRAVELLED WIDELY. VISITING SEVERAL CITIES IN AFRICA AND IN EUROPE, ESPECIALLY PARIS. FOR HUGHES, HOWEVER, THERE WAS NO PLACE LIKE HOME. AND HOME FOR HIM SOON BECAME HARLEM, FOLLOWING A BRIEF STINT IN 1925 IN WASHINGTON AS A BUSBOY IN THE WARDMAN PARK HOTEL WHERE HUGHES WAS "DISCOVERED" BY THE POET VACHEL LINDSAY. AS THE SCHOLAR R. BAXTER MILLER RECOUNTS THE INCIDENT: "ONE AFTERNOON HUGHES PUT COPIES OF HIS POEMS, 'JAZZONIA,' 'NEGRO DANCER' AND 'THE WEARY BLUES,' BESIDE LINDSAY'S DINNER PLATE AND WENT AWAY. ON HIS WAY TO WORK THE NEXT DAY, HUGHES READ IN THE HEADLINES THAT LINDSAY HAD DISCOVERED A 'NEGRO BUSBOY POET.'"

IN TRUTH, HOWEVER, HUGHES WAS ALREADY A HIGHLY RESPECTED POET BY THE TIME HE MET LINDSAY. IN THAT SAME YEAR, ALFRED A. KNOPF, THE WELL-KNOWN EDITOR, BECAME HUGHES'S PUBLISHER, OFFERING HIM A CONTRACT FOR HIS FIRST VOLUME OF POEMS, WHICH WAS PUBLISHED IN 1926 AS "THE WEARY BLUES." A SECOND VOLUME-"FINE CLOTHES TO THE JEW"-FOLLOWED A YEAR LATER. HUGHES WROTE ABOUT BLACK EVERYMAN AND HARLEM WAS HIS HOME. HUGHES WOULD BE TO HARLEM WHAT PUSHKIN WAS TO RUSSIA - ITS VOICE, THE MOMENT OR POINT OF LYRICAL ARTICULATION OF ITS "ZEITGEIST," OF ITS SENSE OF

PLACE, OF THE CONSCIOUSNESS OF THOSE WHO OFTEN COULD NOT ARTICU-
LATE THAT CONSCIOUSNESS THEMSELVES.

DESPITE HIS LOYALTY TO HARLEM, HOWEVER, HUGHES FREQUENTLY
LEFT HIS HOME FOR EXTENSIVE PERIODS, TRAVELLING IN 1931 ON A
ROSENWALD GRANT TO BLACK COLLEGES IN THE SOUTH, SPENDING A
SUMMER IN HAITI, VISITING RUSSIA FOR A YEAR IN 1932 AS PART OF A
FILM COMPANY, THEN RETURNING TO CARMEL, CALIFORNIA, FOR A YEAR,
VIA CHINA AND JAPAN. AS A CORRESPONDENT FOR THE "BALTIMORE AFRO-
AMERICAN" NEWSPAPER, HE WROTE ABOUT THE SPANISH CIVIL WAR,
MEETING IN MADRID SUCH WRITERS AS ERNEST HEMINGWAY, LILLIAN
HELLMAN, ANDRE MALRAUX, PABLO NERUDA AND STEPHEN SPENDER.
BUT INEVITABLY, HE RETURNED TO HARLEM. DURING WORLD WAR II, HE
BEGAN TO WRITE A WEEKLY COLUMN FOR "THE CHICAGO DEFENDER" NEWS-
PAPER, RECOUNTING THE HUMOROUS TALES OF HIS CHARACTER, JESSE B.
SIMPLE, AN URBAN STREET PHILOSOPHER THROUGH WHOM HUGHES WAS
ABLE, FINALLY, TO REACH HUNDREDS OF THOUSANDS OF WORKING CLASS
BLACK AMERICANS. HUGHES WROTE THE WEEKLY COLUMN FOR 20 YEARS
AND PUBLISHED FIVE COLLECTIONS OF HIS "SIMPLE" ESSAYS.

AFTER 1960, HUGHES VISITED SEVERAL OF THE NEWLY INDEPENDENT
AFRICAN COUNTRIES ON BEHALF OF THE STATE DEPARTMENT, WHICH HAD
VIEWED HUGHES SOMEWHAT SUSPICIOUSLY AT LEAST SINCE 1953, WHEN
HE WAS FORCED TO TESTIFY AT THE McCARTHY HEARINGS. WHEN HE
DIED IN 1967, AT THE HEIGHT OF THE BLACK POWER MOVEMENT AND THE
SUCCESSFUL COMPLETION OF THE CIVIL RIGHTS MOVEMENT, HUGHES
HAD LONG BEEN REGARDED AS THE POET LAUREATE OF THE AFRICAN-
AMERICAN PEOPLE.

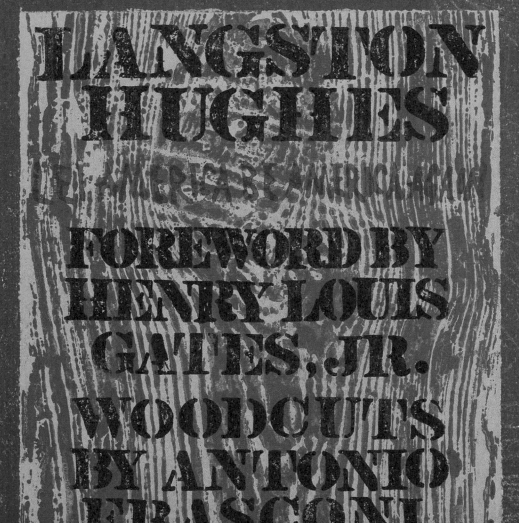

LANGSTON HUGHES

THE AMERICAS AMERICAN POET

FOREWORD BY HENRY LOUIS GATES, JR.

WOODCUTS BY ANTONIO FRASCONI

LET AMERICA BE AMERICA AGAIN
LET IT BE THE DREAM IT USED TO BE
LET IT BE THE PIONEER ON THE PLAIN
SEEKING A HOME WHERE HE
HIMSELF IS FREE

(AMERICA NEVER WAS AMERICA TO ME)

LET AMERICA BE THE DREAM THE
        DREAMERS DREAMED —
LET IT BE THAT GREAT STRONG LAND OF LOVE
WHERE NEVER KINGS CONNIVE OR TYRANTS
                            SCHEME
THAT ANY MAN BE CRUSHED BY ONE ABOVE.

(IT NEVER WAS AMERICA TO ME.)

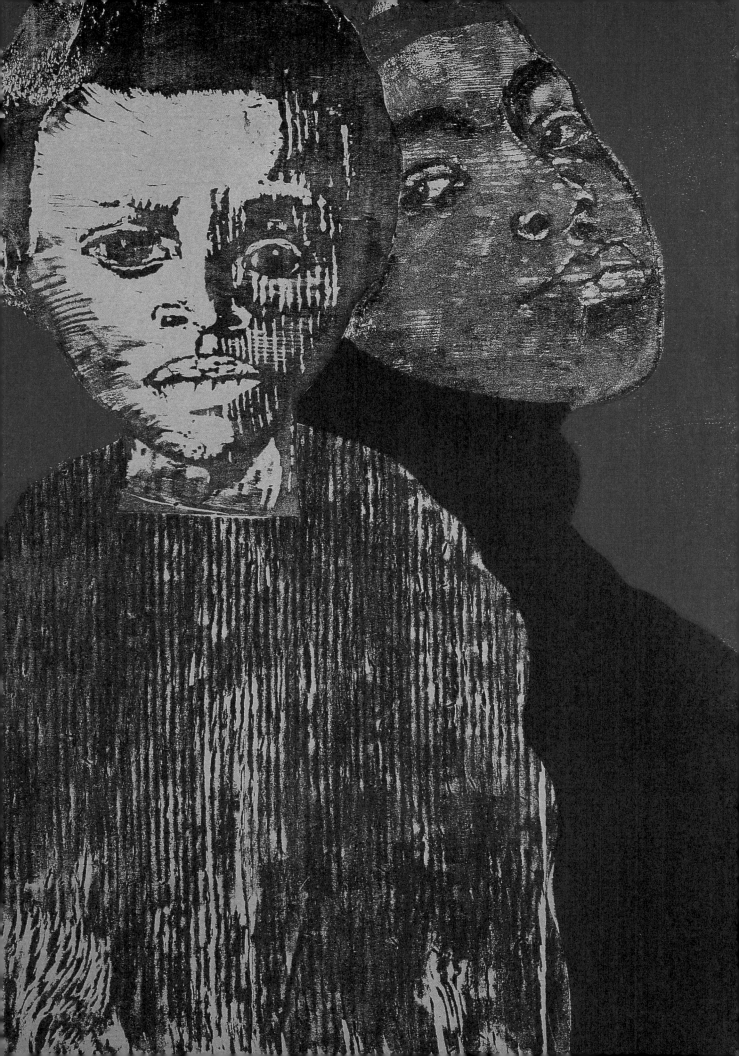

O, LET MY LAND BE A LAND WHERE LIBERTY
IS CROWNED WITH NO FALSE
PATRIOTIC WREATH,
BUT OPPORT   IS REAL AND
                LIFE IS FREE
EQUALITY IS IN   AIR   BREATHE

(THERE'S NEVER BEEN EQUALITY
NOR FREEDOM IN THIS "HOMELAND OF THE FREE"

SAY WHO ARE YOU THAT MUMBLES
              IN THE DARK?
AND WHO ARE YOU THAT DRAWS
YOUR VEIL ACROSS THE STARS?

I AM THE POOR WHITE, FOOLED AND PUSHED APART
I AM THE NEGRO BEARING SLAVERY'S SCAR
I AM THE RED MAN DRIVEN FROM THE LAND
I AM THE IMMIGRANT CLUTCHING THE HOPE
                                                    I SEEK—
AND FINDING ONLY THE SAME OLD STUPID PLAN
OF DOG EAT DOG, OF MIGHTY CRUSH THE WEAK

I AM THE YOUNG MAN, FULL OF STRENGTH
AND HOPE,
TANGLED IN THAT ANCIENT ENDLESS
CHAIN
OF PROFIT, POWER, GAIN, OF GRAB THE LAND!
OF GRAB THE GOLD!
OF GRAB THE WAYS OF SATISFYING NEED!
OF WORK THE MEN! OF TAKE THE PAY!
OF OWNING EVERYTHING FOR ONE'S
OWN GREED!

I AM THE FARMER, BONDSMAN TO THE SOIL.
I AM THE WORKER SOLD TO THE
MACHINE
I AM THE NEGRO, SERVANT TO YOU ALL.
I AM THE PEOPLE, WORRIED HUNGRY, MEAN—
HUNGRY YET TODAY DESPITE THE DREAM
BEATEN YET TODAY—O, PIONEERS!
I AM THE MAN WHO NEVER GOT AHEAD
THE POOREST WORKER BARTERED THROUGH
THE YEARS.

YET I'M THE ONE WHO DREAMT OUR BASIC DREAM
IN THAT OLD WORLD WHILE STILL A SERF OF KINGS,
WHO DREAMT A DREAM SO STRONG, SO BRAVE,
SO TRUE,
THAT EVEN YET ITS MIGHTY DARING SINGS
IN EVERY BRICK AND STONE, IN EVERY
FURROW TURNED
THAT'S MADE AMERICA THE LAND IT HAS BECOME
O, I'M THE MAN WHO SAILED THOSE EARLY SEAS
IN SEARCH OF WHAT I MEANT TO BE MY HOME—
FOR I'M THE ONE WHO LEFT DARK IRELAND'S
AND POLAND'S PLAIN, AND ENGLAND'S
SHORE
AND TORN FROM BLACK GRASSY LEA,
AFRICA'S
TO BUILD A "HOMELAND OF THE FREE."
STRAND I CAME

THE FREE?

A DREAM —

STILL BECKONING TO ME!

O, LET AMERICA BE AMERICA AGAIN
THE LAND THAT NEVER HAS BEEN YET
AND YET MUST BE—
THE LAND WHERE EVERY MAN IS FREE,
THE LAND THAT'S MINE—
THE POOR MAN'S, INDIAN'S, NEGRO'S
ME—

WHO MADE AMERICA,
WHOSE SWEAT AND
BLOOD, WHOSE FAITH
AND PAIN,
WHOSE HAND AT THE FOUNDRY
WHOSE PLOW IN THE RAIN,
MUST BRING BACK OUR
MIGHTY DREAM AGAIN.
SURE, CALL ME ANY UGLY NAME
YOU CHOOSE—
THE STEEL OF FREEDOM
DOES NOT STAIN
FROM THOSE WHO LIVE LIKE
LEECHES ON THE PEOPLES LIVE
WE MUST TAKE BACK OUR
LAND AGAIN
AMERICA!

O, YES,
I SAY IT PLAIN,
AMERICA NEVER WAS AMERICA TO ME,
AND YET I SWEAR THIS OATH
AMERICA WILL BE!
AN EVER-LIVING SEED,
ITS DREAM
LIES DEEP IN THE HEART OF ME.

125t

MY THANKS TO HAROLD OBER ASSOCIATES
FOR PERMISSION TO USE LANGSTON HUGHES'S
POEM. TO PROFESSOR HENRY LOUIS GATES, JR.
FOR HIS FOREWORD, AND TO MS. NORMA
HOWARD OF THE LIBRARY AT PURCHASE
COLLEGE, SUNY, FOR RELATED MATERIAL.

FOR THEIR SUPPORT OF THIS PROJECT, MY
THANKS TO THE POLLOCK-KRASNER
FOUNDATION AND TO THE ROCKEFELLER
FOUNDATION-BELLAGIO STUDY CENTER.
ALSO, MY APPRECIATION TO PURCHASE
COLLEGE FOR TRAVEL SUPPORT, AND
DR. JUDITH KORNBERG FOR PROJECT
ADMINISTRATIVE SUPPORT. WITHOUT
THEIR SUPPORT AND ASSISTANCE, THIS
PROJECT COULD NOT HAVE BEEN COMPLETED.

THIS EDITION IS COMPRISED OF THIRTY
TWO MULTIPLE COLOR WOODCUTS AND
TEXT IN AN EDITION OF FIVE COPIES.
ALL IMAGES AND TEXT ARE CUT AND
PRINTED BY THE ARTIST FROM THE
ORIGINAL BLOCKS ON TROYA PAPER
MOUNTED ONTO ARCHES COVER PAPER,
DURING 1997 AND 1998.

THE EDITION CONSISTS OF FIVE BOUND
COPIES CONTAINING 32 PAGES, 22 1/4
X 15 INCHES, BOUND BY JILL SCHREIBER,
PLUS A SEPARATE EDITION OF FIVE
COPIES PRINTED ON RIVES PAPER.

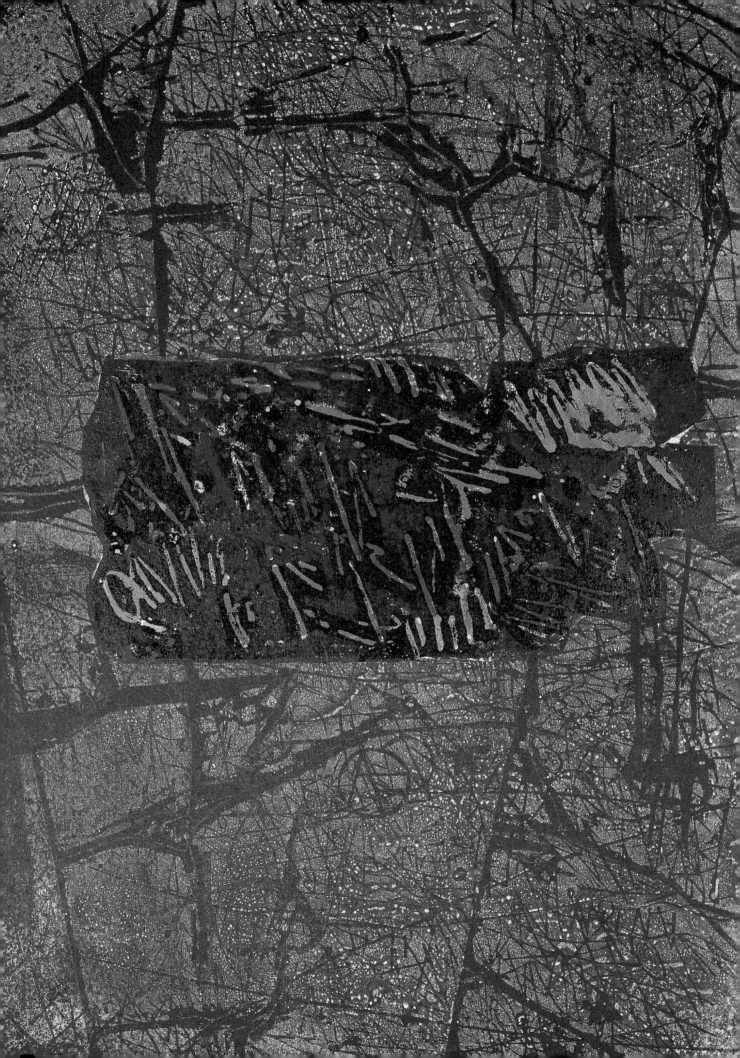

LET AMERICA BE
AMERICA AGAIN

LET AMERICA BE AMERICA AGAIN
LET IT BE THE DREAM IT USED TO BE
LET IT BE THE PIONEER ON THE PLAIN
SEEKING A HOME WHERE HE
                    HIMSELF IS FREE
(AMERICA NEVER WAS AMERICA TO ME)

LET AMERICA BE THE DREAM THE
                    DREAMERS DREAMED —
LET IT BE THAT GREAT STRONG LAND OF LOVE
WHERE NEVER KINGS CONNIVE OR TYRANTS
                                    SCHEME
THAT ANY MAN BE CRUSHED BY ONE ABOVE.
(IT NEVER WAS AMERICA TO ME.)

O, LET MY LAND BE A LAND WHERE
                    LIBERTY
IS CROWNED WITH NO FALSE
                    PATRIOTIC WREATH,
BUT OPPORTUNITY IS REAL, AND
                    LIFE IS FREE,
EQUALITY IS IN THE AIR WE BREATHE.

(THERE'S NEVER BEEN EQUALITY FOR ME
NOR FREEDOM IN THIS "HOMELAND OF THE FREE")

SAY WHO ARE YOU THAT MUMBLES
                    IN THE DARK ?
AND WHO ARE YOU THAT DRAWS
YOUR VEIL ACROSS THE STARS ?

I AM THE POOR WHITE, FOOLED AND PUSHED APART,
I AM THE NEGRO BEARING SLAVERY'S SCARS.
I AM THE RED MAN DRIVEN FROM THE LAND,
I AM THE IMMIGRANT CLUTCHING THE HOPE
                    I SEEK—

AND FINDING ONLY THE SAME OLD STUPID PLAN
OF DOG EAT DOG, OF MIGHTY CRUSH THE WEAK.

I AM THE YOUNG MAN, FULL OF STRENGTH
AND HOPE,
TANGLED IN THAT ANCIENT ENDLESS
CHAIN
OF PROFIT, POWER, GAIN, OF GRAB THE LAND!

OF GRAB THE GOLD!
OF GRAB THE WAYS OF SATISFYING NEED!
OF WORK THE MEN! OF TAKE THE PAY!
OF OWNING EVERYTHING FOR ONE'S
OWN GREED!

I AM THE FARMER, BONDSMAN TO THE SOIL,
I AM THE WORKER SOLD TO THE
MACHINE
I AM THE NEGRO, SERVANT TO YOU ALL,
I AM THE PEOPLE, WORRIED, HUNGRY, MEAN—
HUNGRY YET TODAY DESPITE THE DREAM.
BEATEN YET TODAY—O, PIONEERS!

I AM THE MAN WHO NEVER GOT AHEAD,
THE POOREST WORKER BARTERED THROUGH
THE YEARS.

YET I'M THE ONE WHO DREAMT OUR BASIC DREAM
IN THAT OLD WORLD WHILE STILL A SERF OF KINGS,
WHO DREAMT A DREAM SO STRONG, SO BRAVE,
SO TRUE,
THAT EVEN YET ITS MIGHTY DARING SINGS
IN EVERY BRICK AND STONE, IN EVERY
FURROW TURNED
THAT'S MADE AMERICA THE LAND IT HAS BECOME

O, I'M THE MAN WHO SAILED THOSE EARLY SEAS
IN SEARCH OF WHAT I MEANT TO BE MY HOME—
FOR I'M THE ONE WHO LEFT DARK IRELAND'S
SHORE,
AND POLAND'S PLAIN, AND ENGLAND'S
GRASSY LEA,
AND TORN FROM BLACK AFRICA'S

STRAND I CAME
TO BUILD A "HOMELAND OF THE FREE."

THE FREE?

A DREAM—
STILL BECKONING TO ME!

O, LET AMERICA BE AMERICA AGAIN—
THE LAND THAT NEVER HAS BEEN YET—
AND YET MUST BE—
THE LAND WHERE EVERY MAN IS FREE,
THE LAND THAT'S MINE —

THE POOR MAN'S, INDIAN'S, NEGRO'S ME

WHO MADE AMERICA,
WHOSE SWEAT AND
BLOOD, WHOSE FAITH
AND PAIN,
WHOSE HAND AT THE FOUNDRY,

WHOSE PLOW IN THE RAIN,
MUST BRING BACK OUR
MIGHTY DREAM AGAIN.
SURE, CALL ME ANY UGLY NAME
YOU CHOOSE—

THE STEEL OF FREEDOM
DOES NOT STAIN
FROM THOSE WHO LIVE LIKE
LEECHES ON THE PEOPLE'S LIVES,
WE MUST TAKE BACK OUR
LAND AGAIN.
AMERICA!

O, YES,
I SAY IT PLAIN,
AMERICA NEVER WAS AMERICA TO ME,
AND YET I SWEAR THIS OATH
AMERICA WILL BE!
AN EVER-LIVING SEED,
ITS DREAM

LIES DEEP IN THE HEART OF ME.

WE, THE PEOPLE, MUST REDEEM
OUR LAND, THE MINES, THE PLANTS,
THE RIVERS,

THE MOUNTAINS AND THE ENDLESS
PLAIN —
ALL, ALL THE STRETCH OF THESE
GREAT GREEN STATES
AND MAKE AMERICA AGAIN!

Langston Hughes

LANGSTON HUGHES

Even before the 1926 publication of his first book of poems, *The Weary Blues*, Langston Hughes had earned the title, bestowed upon him by Carl Van Vechten, of "the Negro Poet Laureate." His success in writings other than poetry made him, as he is often called, "the O. Henry of Harlem." Born in Joplin, Missouri, in 1902, he knew a succession of homes in Mexico City; Topeka; Colorado Springs; Charlestown, Indiana; Kansas City; and Buffalo. He graduated from Central High School in Cleveland, worked for a time there and in Chicago, and finally went on to New York where he studied for a year at Columbia University. His best school was the world, in which he traveled widely and well, bringing together in his varied and colorful writings the experiences of a profitably restless life. He died in 1967, in New York.

ANTONIO FRASCONI

Born in 1919, Antonio Frasconi grew up in Montevideo, Uruguay. He emigrated to the United States to study at the Art Students' League and later attended and taught at the New School for Social Research. Throughout his career as a printmaker specializing in woodcuts, Frasconi has published hundreds of prints and folios and has illustrated many books, including art and children's books. Frasconi's work ranges from landscapes to images on social and racial issues. The scope of his work can be seen in *Frasconi: Against the Grain; The Woodcuts of Antonio Frasconi* and *Kaleidoscope in Woodcuts*. Examples of his illustrations can be seen in Pablo Neruda's *Bestiary / Bestiario* and *A Whitman Portrait*. Frasconi has taught at the Brooklyn Museum School, the Atlanta Art Institute, and the State University of New York at Purchase, where he is an emeritus professor. He lives in Norwalk, Connecticut.

HENRY LOUIS GATES, JR.

An editor, writer, critic, and lecturer, Henry Louis Gates, Jr. is the author of several works of literary criticism, including *Figures in Black: Words, Signs and the Racial Self* and *The Signifying Monkey: A Theory of Afro-American Literary Criticism*, winner of the 1989 American Book Award. Selected as one of *Time* magazine's Twenty-Five Most Influential Americans, he is Chairperson of Harvard University's Afro-American Studies Department, as well as W. E. B. Du Bois Professor of the Humanities and Director of the W. E. B. Du Bois Institute of Afro-American Research.